To the world's
neighbor...

John Edmund
Psalm 91

365

THINGS
EVERY
SUCCESSFUL
LEADER
SHOULD
KNOW

JOHN EDMUND
HAGGAI

HARVEST HOUSE PUBLISHERS

EUGENE, OREGON

Cover by Dugan Design Group, Bloomington, Minnesota

365 THINGS EVERY SUCCESSFUL LEADER SHOULD KNOW
Copyright © 2010 by John Edmund Haggai
Published by Harvest House Publishers
Eugene, Oregon 97402
www.harvesthousepublishers.com

ISBN 978-0-7369-2940-0

Printed in the United States of America

10 11 12 13 14 15 16 17 18 / BP-SK / 10 9 8 7 6 5 4 3 2 1

INTRODUCTION

∞

For over seven decades, writing has occupied the center ground of my life and thought.

Lord Bacon said, "Writing makes an exact man."

He spoke the truth.

Writing produces exactitude by forcing you to set down ideas in logical relation to one another. Writing crystallizes your thoughts and makes your ideas specific.

At crucial times, I have locked myself away from human company in order to write.

The globe-encircling ministry of Haggai Institute took shape in the Bali Beach Intercontinental Hotel. I shut the door to my room and applied myself single-mindedly to the business of committing my thoughts to paper. For two days I did nothing but scribble on a yellow legal pad.

Later I devoted four years to writing a book that contains the basis of my thinking about leadership.

Writing matters. It is the most potent way in which language can transmit invisible thoughts from one mind to another.

So when Bob Hawkins Jr. of Harvest House Publishers suggested that I bring together a distillation of ideas on leadership for this volume, I immediately agreed.

The words on the following pages come from a range of my books and writings, including the private circular *Notes From My Diary*, which I send only to a group of close associates.

Beyond that, these words are rooted in more than a hundred journeys around the world, innumerable meetings with the world's truly great leaders, and decades of personal reflection and application.

Each thought in the pages that follow is a tiny lens through which you will see more clearly the quality and direction of your own leadership.

Each page will cost you just sixty seconds of reading and reflection. Some may keep you thinking to the end of the day. Some—as I have found—you may still be wrestling with to the end of your life.

Attempt something so great for God,
it's doomed to failure unless God be in it.

HAGGAI'S LAWS

Leadership is the discipline of
deliberately exerting special influence
within a group to move it toward
goals of beneficial permanence that
fulfill the group's real needs.

THE INFLUENTIAL LEADER

Hurry is symptomatic of a
weakly organized mind.

HOW TO WIN OVER WORRY

4

Today's attitude is tomorrow's reality.

HAGGAI'S LAWS

When I first talked about goal setting, I laid great emphasis on making the goals realistic. Only a couple of years ago, after a lifetime of setting goals, did it occur to me that I'd never set a realistic goal in my life.

THE INFLUENTIAL LEADER

Worry is a time thief.

HOW TO WIN OVER WORRY

Have you ever had an idea that's so
obvious, so simple, that you thought:
*If there were any value in this, surely
someone would have acted on it by now?*

THE LEADING EDGE

Givers enjoy talking about giving.

NOTES FROM MY DIARY

9

The effective speaker has something
worthy to say and says it worthily.

THE INFLUENTIAL LEADER

10

Time is more than money; time
is life. When you waste it, you
destroy part of your life.

THE STEWARD

11

Negative thoughts and fears
become self-fulfilling prophecies.

HOW TO WIN OVER WORRY

12

One cannot lead an army from
behind a desk. Nothing takes
the place of face-to-face.

NOTES FROM MY DIARY

13

A God-given vision is an awesome
responsibility. Fulfillment can lead you
to the heights of tremendous service
to God and your fellow man. Failure
to follow the vision will deprive
others of the leadership they need.

THE INFLUENTIAL LEADER

14

God does not look for perfection.
He looks for obedience.

NOTES FROM MY DIARY

15

Goals simplify the decision-making process. Goals tone up mental and physical health. Goals generate respect. Goals provide a system of measure so you may enjoy the feeling of accomplishment. Goals produce persistence. And goals, under God, deliver the leader from bondage to the plaudits of people.

THE INFLUENTIAL LEADER

16

Shape the way you think by what you do.

HAGGAI'S LAWS

17

Love is not a sentimental emotion but an
act of the will in which a leader works
toward the highest good of others.

THE INFLUENTIAL LEADER

18

The most difficult sin for Christians to
overcome is the sin of financial dishonesty.

NOTES FROM MY DIARY

19

Your influence for God rests
squarely on your ability to create
and cultivate friendship.

HAGGAI'S LAWS

20

Leaders without vision are like guides
without a map. Though they may
come across as strong, confident, and
independent, in reality they are not
influencers but "influencees."

THE INFLUENTIAL LEADER

21

Criticism has taught me a lot more than
praise. I prefer praise, but I profit from
criticism—even when it is unjust.

NOTES FROM MY DIARY

22

A large gift is a gift of any size into which
the sacrificial spirit has been introduced.

THE STEWARD

23

If you don't have the luxury of vacations
where you can get away from others,
find ways of creating your own solitude.
Find time at the beginning of the day
to do your undisturbed thinking. Or
cultivate your own inner solitude
even in the midst of a noisy crowd.

THE INFLUENTIAL LEADER

24

Don't leave your mind open to the
negative influence of other people.

HOW TO WIN OVER WORRY

25

Since you're conditioned by your
environment, create the environment
that moves you to your goals.

HAGGAI'S LAWS

26

Give the Lord the first part of each
day, the first day of each week, and
the first tenth of your income.

THE STEWARD

27

What two individuals achieve
separately can be achieved faster,
better, and more enjoyably if those
two individuals work together.

THE WACKERSBERG CONNECTION

28

The celebrated financier John Templeton
once told me that "a leader must encourage
change." He must not simply tolerate or
accept it, but actually encourage it. At the
time, Templeton was seventy years old.

HOW TO WIN OVER WORRY

29

On average I'd say my investment in relationships takes up something like twenty hours a week. And that's not cold-calling potential donors or drumming up business. That's just maintaining a portfolio of existing friendships.

THE SEVEN SECRETS OF SUCCESSFUL
BUSINESS RELATIONSHIPS

30

The unrepentant sinner will go to hell, but he'll leave earth with a better financial statement than the nontithing believer! An atheist who plants a thousand acres of corn will get a bigger crop than the believer who plants one acre! It's a matter of sowing and reaping. The law of gravity does not distinguish between saints and sinners. Nor does tithing.

NOTES FROM MY DIARY

31

Without scheduling and organization
you will move fast and make mistakes.

HOW TO WIN OVER WORRY

32

The successful investor focuses his
attention on the possible return, not
on what other investors are doing.

NOTES FROM MY DIARY

33

Put your money where you
want your heart to be.

THE WACKERSBERG CONNECTION

34

Let the Dow Jones soar 150 points in
one day, and one looks in vain to find
a bear. Let it drop 250 points in one
day, and it's hard to find many bulls.

NOTES FROM MY DIARY

35

If you plan no changes in your life, in five years you'll be the same person you are now—or less. Does that fact motivate you? It should. God does not merely wish you to make a difference. He does not merely hope for you to make a difference. He commands it. He tells you to go out there and change things, globally, exponentially.

EXPONENTIAL

36

Love involves the totality of one's being.
It involves unconquerable consideration,
charitableness, and benevolence. It
means that, no matter what anyone
does to you in the way of humiliation,
abuse, or injury, you work toward that
person's highest good. That amounts
to a tough requirement—and one
that few leaders can claim to fulfill.

THE INFLUENTIAL LEADER

37

Man and woman can never be spectators
to their own marriage. They must
be participants, protagonists and
antagonists alike. They may succumb
to the abrasions of their relationship
and settle for a discordant union. Or
together they may build, lesson upon
lesson, success against failure, caring
and sharing, loving and learning.

MY SON JOHNNY

38

"Oh Lord, help me to be everything
I shall wish I had been when I
stand in Your presence. Amen."

NOTES FROM MY DIARY

39

Prayer is the means whereby we
make contact with God's strength.

HOW TO WIN OVER WORRY

40

Influential leadership, by which I mean
broadly leadership that changes the world
for good, consists of decisions, big and
small, that all derive their inspiration
and direction from a single life aim.

THE INFLUENTIAL LEADER

41

If someone doesn't enjoy doing business with you—it doesn't matter who you are—as soon as someone else comes down the pike with a product or service as good as yours, he'll take his business to that other person. At the end of the day, it's just that simple. So it's good business to relate well. In fact, it's stupidity not to.

THE SEVEN SECRETS OF SUCCESSFUL
BUSINESS RELATIONSHIPS

42

Observe the same clear rules of honest dealing in your transactions with God that you consider imperative in your dealings with your fellow men.

THE STEWARD

43

Has it ever occurred to you that
the people who are in the greatest
need of prayer are those who do not
know even to ask for prayer?

EXPONENTIAL

44

As long as you go on hating your
enemies, you are giving them the
sovereignty of your own life. You are
literally forcing them to dominate you.

HOW TO WIN OVER WORRY

45

Leadership transcends all forms
of organization. People talk about
"business leadership" and "political
leadership" and "military leadership."
Yet the fundamentals underlying good
leadership have nothing to do with the
specifics of business or politics or warfare.
Leadership is a discipline in itself and
can be applied with equal effectiveness
to any organization and any purpose.

THE INFLUENTIAL LEADER

46

A single introduction, a single word, a
single piece of well-chosen advice can
influence the entire world for good.

THE WACKERSBERG CONNECTION

47

Does a relationship with Jesus mean you'll
never be in financial or physical danger?
Not at all. But it does mean freedom from
fear and the promise of Him who says,
"I will never leave you nor forsake you."

NOTES FROM MY DIARY

48

God trusts you because of the
indwelling Holy Spirit within you.

EXPONENTIAL

49

Decision making sits at the heart of
leadership. In fact, leadership really boils
down to a constant execution of decisions,
big and small, day in, day out. And the
trail of decisions a leader leaves behind
him charts the trajectory of his influence.

THE INFLUENTIAL LEADER

50

Quite simply, Jesus says, the secret
of financial freedom is to practice
the biblical mandate of giving.

10 COMMANDMENTS FOR FINANCIAL
FREEDOM AND CRISIS SURVIVAL

51

God gives us children as life's
supreme investment.

MY SON JOHNNY

52

Many people can brood for fifteen
minutes. They can worry for fifteen
minutes. But very few people can focus
their attention on any given (and, I might
add, worthwhile) subject for fifteen
minutes. Almost without exception,
after two minutes their minds will
have drifted onto something else.

HOW TO WIN OVER WORRY

53

No one can think outside the
parameters of his or her vocabulary.

NOTES FROM MY DIARY

54

If you are a Christian believer in an
unbelieving society, you are a leader. Let
me say that again: to be a Christian in
secular society is to be a leader, full stop.
You may or may not occupy a leadership
position in a Christian organization or
the business world. But even if you feel
no special calling and hold no position of
responsibility, the burden of leading others
to salvation falls directly on your shoulders.

THE INFLUENTIAL LEADER

55

There's no rule that says our friendships have to arise by accident. We have no difficulty with the idea of targeting potential mates. Why should it bother us to target potential friends?

THE SEVEN SECRETS OF SUCCESSFUL
BUSINESS RELATIONSHIPS

56

It takes courage to develop your abilities—
it's easier to bask in the warm atmosphere
of the comfort zone and risk nothing.

THE STEWARD

57

We are seeing a global crisis of leadership, a crisis brought about by a rapid expansion of world population and the fact that too many in leadership positions treat leadership as a technical skill, not as a discipline deeply rooted in faith and character.

THE INFLUENTIAL LEADER

58

Nobody has it all. In my experience, everybody's got at least one major problem and most have more than one.

NOTES FROM MY DIARY

59

You invest your influence into the
lives of others to attain—faster and
more efficiently—common objectives
of mutual desire and benefit.

BE CAREFUL WHAT YOU
CALL IMPOSSIBLE

60

A true friend maintains relationships,
stays in touch—even when he or she
has moved to a distant city or years
have passed since face-to-face contact.

THE WACKERSBERG CONNECTION

61

Leadership is something you do. The success or failure of your career, in business or the pastorate, will one day be judged by the quality of the decisions you made. They may be mundane and pragmatic decisions. Or they may be visionary decisions. It's up to you to decide.

THE INFLUENTIAL LEADER

62

The church is the only business that stays in business after it has gone out of business.

NOTES FROM MY DIARY

63

God calls us to overreach ourselves because
His reach is so much longer than ours.

EXPONENTIAL

64

The great world Christian, John Wesley,
appreciated the value of time. For fifty-
two years he kept an account of how
he had spent every fifteen-minute
period of his waking hours. Once
while waiting for a delayed carriage
to take him to an appointment, he
said, "I have lost ten minutes forever."

THE STEWARD

65

If God takes you seriously enough
to entrust you with a vision, then
you must take yourself seriously.

THE INFLUENTIAL LEADER

66

If you know something's going wrong,
admit it. After all, business boils down
to problem solving. No one's going to get
angry at you for admitting you need help.
They will get angry at you—and with
some justification—if you let a problem
get out of hand by refusing to consult,
or if you fail to keep others informed.

THE SEVEN SECRETS OF SUCCESSFUL
BUSINESS RELATIONSHIPS

67

Yesterday is a cashed check and cannot
be negotiated. Tomorrow is a promissory
note and cannot yet be utilized. Today
is cash in hand. Spend it wisely.

HOW TO WIN OVER WORRY

68

Too many parents want to be pals
with their children and grandchildren
instead of leading them.

NOTES FROM MY DIARY

69

Leader and vision are inextricably linked.
They cannot be separated. Part of realizing
a vision is realizing your own potential to
pursue that vision and see it bear fruit. If
a leader has a vision, but does not take
his own potential seriously, that vision
will soon die. It will remain a dream.

THE INFLUENTIAL LEADER

70

Anyone who's had an impossible
problem will know how tempting it is
to just sit there and stare at it. As long
as you are staring at the problem with
its long shadow of dismal consequences,
you are no nearer a solution.

BE CAREFUL WHAT YOU
CALL IMPOSSIBLE

71

The fact is, most people will like you
when you're cheerful, and if you're
miserable, most people won't.

THE WACKERSBERG CONNECTION

72

You're never going to move into a
new elevation for God—into a new
height, a new usefulness—if you are
not willing to dismantle something.

NOTES FROM MY DIARY

73

I don't subjugate my dreams to
memories; that's a sure route to failure.

EXPONENTIAL

74

But God will work through you,
in spite of all your inadequacies, if you
only have faith in His power. God never
assigns a task and then deprives His agent
of the tools required to complete it.

THE INFLUENTIAL LEADER

75

Your genuine interest in other people
will assassinate the monster of worry.

HOW TO WIN OVER WORRY

76

People do business with people.
Being competent in relationships
is the fundamental skill.

THE SEVEN SECRETS OF SUCCESSFUL
BUSINESS RELATIONSHIPS

Visions don't require experience. They don't require academic degrees. The key word is potential. Your vision may take you into an area you have never been in before. You will need to learn new skills. What matters, then, is not what you know already, but how much confidence and self-belief you have based on your faith in God.

THE INFLUENTIAL LEADER

78

Expect ingratitude.

HOW TO WIN OVER WORRY

79

Smiling may not be the most complex management technique, yet an infectious smile exerts a powerful influence on business relationships. People who smile easily seem more likeable. This helps in the conduct of more effective business transactions.

THE SEVEN SECRETS OF SUCCESSFUL BUSINESS RELATIONSHIPS

80

When you answer criticism volcanically,
you lose possession of many of your
faculties. Your thoughts become
inaccurate, your decisions unwise,
and your words regrettable.

HOW TO WIN OVER WORRY

81

Without wholehearted and realistic
commitment to a vision, you will
never see it through, and you will
never practice real leadership. You may
occupy a leadership position. But you
will not be an influential leader.

THE INFLUENTIAL LEADER

82

The measure of worth is not net worth, not recognition, not being voted one of the twenty-five most important Americans, not inclusion in the international Who's Who, not exercising secular power over the lives of people reduced almost to serfdom, not engaging in the merry-go-round of pleasure. The only measure of worth is permanence.

THE STEWARD

83

Since you'll never find a fail-safe way to control your estate from the grave, you need to prayerfully determine the best possible course to distribute now as much as possible for the glory of God.

EXPONENTIAL

84

Free speech will not last long after
effective speech has gone by the board.

NOTES FROM MY DIARY

85

Don't confuse leadership with
management. Though a manager can
keep an operation running, only an
influential leader can motivate people to
accomplish those changes that meet their
real needs. I'm not putting managers
down; the world needs good managers.
Management, though, is not leadership.

THE INFLUENTIAL LEADER

86

You tend to absorb the
characteristics of your environment.

NOTES FROM MY DIARY

87

Concentrating on possible disaster
distorts your thinking and paralyzes
your will. It prohibits those measures
necessary for financial victory.

10 COMMANDMENTS FOR FINANCIAL
FREEDOM AND CRISIS SURVIVAL

88

Nothing comes before the work
of God—not even business.

THE WACKERSBERG CONNECTION

89

Self-control doesn't vanish overnight.
It slips away little by little, under the
constant pressure of an unguarded
lifestyle. Paradoxically, this erosion of self-
control is most likely to happen in those
areas where you think you are strongest
and feel most confident and secure.

THE INFLUENTIAL LEADER

90

Tomorrow's opportunities will be lost
unless we prepare for them today.

MY SON JOHNNY

91

Give attention to every appeal that
comes your way; it may turn out
to be a God-given opportunity.

THE STEWARD

92

If you cannot describe something
as good and honorable, then
refuse to think of it at all.

HOW TO WIN OVER WORRY

93

A goal program is not a wish list; it is a
program of work. In business, visions
should be permanent and goals flexible.
But often it turns out the other way
around. The goals become fixed and vision
lapses. Businesses cling to old buildings,
old markets, old structures—long after
these have fallen into terminal decline.
The market is constantly changing. If you
don't follow the changes by adjusting your
goals, then in financial terms you are dead.

THE INFLUENTIAL LEADER

94

Develop the habit of appreciating people.

THE SEVEN SECRETS OF SUCCESSFUL
BUSINESS RELATIONSHIPS

95

Were it not for my ability to relax,
I would be a physical and emotional
basket case by this time. At an age
that some consider twenty years past
retirement, I thank God I'm still able
to function with a great deal of energy
and zest. The key? The ability to relax.

HOW TO WIN OVER WORRY

96

Faith is visualizing as an accomplished reality the thing for which you are praying.

10 COMMANDMENTS FOR FINANCIAL
FREEDOM AND CRISIS SURVIVAL

97

People depend on you. They often lean on you. When things go badly they complain, and when things go well they don't always remember to credit you or say thanks. In short, being an influential leader will be a constant drain on your resources. Where will you go to refuel yourself?

THE INFLUENTIAL LEADER

98

Consensus thinking is never creative
thinking. In the establishment of
any enterprise, consensus thinking
rarely achieves spectacular results.

EXPONENTIAL

99

A person who will not read is no better
off than one who cannot read.

NOTES FROM MY DIARY

100

Unlike networking, friendship requires you to care for people or for them to care for you. Networking is effective; friendship endures.

THE WACKERSBERG CONNECTION

101

Most folks, when the impossible confronts them, give up before they even try. They don't give themselves the chance to succeed because they've decided in advance that they can't.

BE CAREFUL WHAT YOU
CALL IMPOSSIBLE

102

True contentment springs from the ability
to put your own concerns second, and
to express love for others by giving.

THE INFLUENTIAL LEADER

103

Most people say, "I want to be remembered
as one who made a difference." Well, no
Christian would disagree with that, but
what kind of a difference do you want
to make? Have you planned it in your
mind? Have you worked out the details
of how, under God, you're going to
make a lasting and a godly impact?

EXPONENTIAL

104

The man who knows
everything learns nothing.

THE INFLUENTIAL LEADER

105

No great work has ever been done without
enthusiasm. Look around you at the
great leaders of industry, the great media
figures, the great sports personalities.
Without exception, they are driven by
enthusiasm. They focus on the one thing
that motivates them, and the power of that
motivation emerges in high performance.

HOW TO WIN OVER WORRY

106

The first question to ask yourself
before you reach for the phone is:
Do I really need to make this call?
As much as half the time (if you're
honest), you'll find the answer is no.

THE SEVEN SECRETS OF SUCCESSFUL
BUSINESS RELATIONSHIPS

107

God never moved the world
through a majority. Rather, the
creative and dedicated minority.

EXPONENTIAL

108

Self-control comes down to successful
leadership of your own character.

THE INFLUENTIAL LEADER

109

Death is characterized by inaction.

HOW TO WIN OVER WORRY

110

What has taken place in your life
that could not have taken place
if there were no Holy Spirit?

THE STEWARD

111

The most persistent command of God
in the Word of God to the people
of God is to evangelize the world.

EXPONENTIAL

112

A friend told me he could not possibly control his temper. He attributed his ungovernable explosions of anger to his parents and grandparents. He said there were some people, like himself, who could not be expected to rule their own spirits. I asked him, "If you were in a heated argument with your wife and someone knocked on your door, would you continue to shout?"

THE INFLUENTIAL LEADER

113

Think out your desired destination at the end of twelve months. Write it out in detail. That is your first step to arriving there sooner than you ever dreamed possible.

NOTES FROM MY DIARY

114

Men or women, wealthy or poor, literate or illiterate, famous or obscure, we all wield influence over others whether we know it or not. We can't avoid it. And if we are wise, we will invest that influence as we would invest money in stocks or bonds or real estate, to exploit to the fullest its potential for accomplishing the good.

THE WACKERSBERG CONNECTION

115

The person who stays immersed in
problems and never focuses on solutions
will never achieve the goals desired.

NOTES FROM MY DIARY

116

How often we respond unthinkingly
to suggestions from outside.

THE INFLUENTIAL LEADER

117

When God puts you in a tough situation—and make no mistake, when you're a believer there's no such thing as blind chance or bad luck—it's so you can grasp the initiative and reap the dividends of obedience.

EXPONENTIAL

118

Thank God for your knowledge of finance. Encourage your advisors. Pray for your head of state and all legislators. But look to God.

10 COMMANDMENTS FOR FINANCIAL
FREEDOM AND CRISIS SURVIVAL

119

Set your goals, lay out your plan of action, make your commitment for fulfilling those goals, look to the Lord for grace and guidance, and decisively move ahead—that's stewardship!

THE STEWARD

120

You are the product of your thoughts. Yet you have the power to determine what you think about. Act on this ability. Deliberately choose the thoughts you have.

THE INFLUENTIAL LEADER

121

Positive thinking needs God. You
might just as well try to shoot an
African lion with a water pistol as try
to conquer worry with a self-inspired
and self-produced positive attitude.

HOW TO WIN OVER WORRY

122

Without a preset time limit, what could be
done in ninety minutes may take six hours.

THE SEVEN SECRETS OF SUCCESSFUL
BUSINESS RELATIONSHIPS

123

Take the initiative in building social contacts—don't wait for others to do it. Call people just so they know you're thinking about them. Be there to lend a helping hand in their hour of need. Be generous with your time and resources.

THE WACKERSBERG CONNECTION

124

People on the receiving end of "the truth"
may have all sorts of reasons for not
accepting it. The medical patient may be
in denial over an alarming diagnosis. The
executive may have locked himself into
his own program or plan. The teenager
may care more about the opinions of
her peers than those of her parents. In
each case, careful explanations and
faultless logic will fall on deaf ears.

THE INFLUENTIAL LEADER

125

I have a hard time understanding how
people can dress better in the office
on Monday morning than they do in
the sanctuary of God on Sunday.

NOTES FROM MY DIARY

126

Obeying the Great Commission—and I
mean obeying it in the terms in which it
was given, not in some emasculated version
we happen to find convenient—is the key
to doing good in the twenty-first century.

EXPONENTIAL

127

When I put up a notice in my study
targeting a certain level of return on my
investments, I'm not just setting a goal.
I'm saying to myself, That's what I want to
attain. Knowing I want it makes me more
willing to expend the effort to get there.

THE SEVEN SECRETS OF SUCCESSFUL
BUSINESS RELATIONSHIPS

128

Listening has become a
hugely underrated skill.

THE INFLUENTIAL LEADER

129

You have no direct control over other people's decision making. Indeed, any attempt at coercion will almost certainly backfire and produce resentment and intransigence. All you can do in motivating others is make as clear a link as possible between the goals you want them to share and the desires that most powerfully drive them.

THE SEVEN SECRETS OF SUCCESSFUL
BUSINESS RELATIONSHIPS

130

Businessmen across the world, petrified
by fear and paralyzed by anxiety over
reverses in their business, could enjoy
business success and more if they
would only surrender themselves to
God and take Him as their partner.

HOW TO WIN OVER WORRY

131

Every Christian believes in God,
but very few give evidence of believing
God. They say, "God will provide
all our needs according to His riches
in glory." But when they look at the
Wall Street Journal or the stock market
pages and the news is negative, their
faces show they don't believe God.

10 COMMANDMENTS FOR FINANCIAL
FREEDOM AND CRISIS SURVIVAL

132

Always distinguish the goal of
gaining consent from the goal
of beating the opposition.

THE INFLUENTIAL LEADER

133

Evangelism capable of reaching every
person on the planet must be able
to reproduce itself exponentially.

EXPONENTIAL

134

Faith works in the realm
of the humanly impossible.

NOTES FROM MY DIARY

135

If you knew you had only thirty more days to live, what would you do? What changes would you make? How would you reallocate your time—and your money?

EXPONENTIAL

136

Force and one-upmanship don't achieve persuasion. You are aiming to have others say "Yes, that's the right way to go," not "Yes, he was right."

THE INFLUENTIAL LEADER

137

Do you stay true to your word, even in small matters? When you keep your promises, you set a pattern of behavior that assures others they can do business with you. Its essence lies in honoring commitments—to yourself, to others, to the organization, to your family, and, fundamentally, to God.

NOTES FROM MY DIARY

138

Free enterprise depends on our ability to form relationships and establish trust—on our ability to invest influence by means of friendship.

THE WACKERSBERG CONNECTION

139

I use the terms investment and giving
interchangeably. In other words, I invest
in numerous ways (time, relationships,
learning, charitable donation)
with exactly the same optimistic
expectation of return as I have when
I make a financial investment.

THE INFLUENTIAL LEADER

140

Get a voice coach.

NOTES FROM MY DIARY

141

You cannot obey God yesterday.
And you have no assurance you can
obey God tomorrow. Your next breath is
in God's hand. Therefore, the question
is: What will be your response today?

EXPONENTIAL

142

Consider your blessings. For how much money would you sell the health God has given to you? How much does your wife's love mean to you? Have you ever thoroughly evaluated the value of your child's devotion? For what amount would you sell your reputation if it could be put on the open market? What premium do you put upon the eyesight God has given you? What about the capacity to hear, and to speak, and to feel, and to taste? Have you ever thought about how impoverished you would be if suddenly you were to be deprived of all your friends?

HOW TO WIN OVER WORRY

143

Without vulnerability, there is
no viability. Without risk, there
is no forward movement.

THE INFLUENTIAL LEADER

144

There is nothing more invigorating
than the awareness of tasks efficiently
completed, and there is nothing
more dispiriting than the knowledge
of unfulfilled responsibilities.

HOW TO WIN OVER WORRY

145

If you have to do something, you
may as well give it all you've got.

THE SEVEN SECRETS OF SUCCESSFUL
BUSINESS RELATIONSHIPS

146

It is often easier to give money to a
beggar than it is to follow up and
see what it is he really needs.

THE STEWARD

147

Keeping your mind on winning the race
is the first step to making it a reality.
Believing a friend can accomplish a
difficult task and telling him he can do it
will help to make that outcome possible.

THE INFLUENTIAL LEADER

148

A poor organization is an organization
led by people who are not capable
of realizing all the opportunities
God puts in their hands.

EXPONENTIAL

149

Take the world for your gymnasium
and godliness for your daily exercise.

NOTES FROM MY DIARY

150

Be careful what you call impossible—
because as soon as you call something
impossible, you make it so.

BE CAREFUL WHAT YOU
CALL IMPOSSIBLE

151

I would rather have the
first-class commitment of a
second-class man than the second-class
commitment of a first-class man.

NOTES FROM MY DIARY

152

If you are short of cash, don't hoard
the little you've got. Give some
away. From a financial standpoint,
it's the best thing you can do.

THE INFLUENTIAL LEADER

153

What has killed vision in more instances
than I can enumerate is the habit
Christians have of determining the price
tag before deciding what God wants.

VITALIZE THE VISION

154

Would I make the same decisions
my employees make? Not always.
Remarkably their decisions yield better
results than some I would have made!

NOTES FROM MY DIARY

155

You can no more serve the next generation
than you can serve the last generation,
except as the Holy Spirit, using your
influence by life and by lip, induces
family, friends, or associates to carry on
your own vision and commitment.

EXPONENTIAL

156

Nobody follows a person who complains.

THE INFLUENTIAL LEADER

157

When you have a problem, jump in the middle of it and work your way out.

THE STEWARD

158

I cannot think of any major first-time approach where I didn't work out in detail what I planned to do—and then pre-played the whole thing. It's amazing how many fidgets, weak gestures, flat phrases, and blank expressions you can catch just by doing a few dry runs in front of a mirror and a tape recorder.

THE SEVEN SECRETS OF SUCCESSFUL BUSINESS RELATIONSHIPS

159

If you worry about the smallest things,
pray about the smallest things.

HOW TO WIN OVER WORRY

160

There are two types of people:
thermometers and thermostats.

THE INFLUENTIAL LEADER

161

The investment of influence can start from anywhere, with anyone, at any scale.

THE WACKERSBERG CONNECTION

162

The majority is nearly always wrong.

HAGGAI'S LAWS

163

God does not test you to break you
down. He does it to prove your worth.
To prove His presence in your life. And
His sufficiency for all your needs.

EXPONENTIAL

164

Those who work with me will testify
that it's not my practice to hover over
them, commenting on their every
move. They get plenty of space.

NOTES FROM MY DIARY

165

Anyone can succeed in ideal conditions.
That kind of success takes no genius.
You demonstrate genius when your
success grows out of failure.

THE INFLUENTIAL LEADER

166

It can be an almost overwhelming
temptation to chip in on a discussion
that doesn't concern you, the effect
of which will almost certainly be
to further obscure the issue.

THE SEVEN SECRETS OF SUCCESSFUL
BUSINESS RELATIONSHIPS

167

Prayer is the best cell phone
you will ever have.

HOW TO WIN OVER WORRY

168

Victorious living requires the
willingness to respond obediently and
quickly to the impulses of the Spirit.
Delayed obedience is disobedience
and not worth half a hallelujah.

NOTES FROM MY DIARY

169

To correct and profit from your mistakes,
you must assume responsibility for them.

THE INFLUENTIAL LEADER

170

God has a marvelous way of achieving
His purposes, but He doesn't always
move in the channels we expect.

NOTES FROM MY DIARY

171

God will not be anyone's debtor.

EXPONENTIAL

172

No amount of money can save a soul, build a character, evangelize a city, or motivate a group of people, yet it is a factor without which these results would not be accomplished.

THE STEWARD

173

Going out for lunch is a waste of time.
If someone has scheduled a lunch with
me, they usually—at my request—
join me in my office. Restaurant or
club personnel don't interrupt, and
the environment lends itself more
to serious and focused conversation.
Also, I can lay hands in seconds on
materials relevant to the discussion.

NOTES FROM MY DIARY

174

Most people decide it's easier to back
out of relationships than to mend
them. But broken relationships leave a
poisonous trail behind them. Influential
leaders keep relationships working.

THE INFLUENTIAL LEADER

175

Your life consists of a series of choices.
And those choices are interwoven with
actions. Until you act in confidence upon
the matter that you say is important
to you, you will never make it.

NOTES FROM MY DIARY

176

I have long been convinced of a
universal law that we attract to
ourselves those people and conditions
compatible with our state of mind.

THE SEVEN SECRETS OF SUCCESSFUL
BUSINESS RELATIONSHIPS

177

How about putting the Lord Jesus in the
middle of your social calendar? How about
inconveniencing yourself, if necessary, in
order to honor Him? How about taking
some time out to read what's going on in
the world so you can pray effectively?

EXPONENTIAL

178

The first step to overcoming your fears
is to identify them and study them.
Something brought into the light of
understanding will lose much of its power.

THE INFLUENTIAL LEADER

179

Focus on results not activity.

HOW TO WIN OVER WORRY

180

I have been blessed by the friendship of
two men who, on hearing a plan, can lay
bare a weakness in it with explosive speed.

THE INFLUENTIAL LEADER

181

Browbeating is not a reliable method
of getting things done on time.

THE SEVEN SECRETS OF SUCCESSFUL
BUSINESS RELATIONSHIPS

182

Remember that the greatest
democrat in the world is death.

NOTES FROM MY DIARY

183

I have so often heard leaders say,
"We need to back off of this project.
God must not be in it. So much
opposition has arisen. It obviates
the possibility of advance." I wonder
what Bible they're reading from—
what version, what language? I do
not find any place in Scripture where
God did a great work and it was not
accompanied by virulent opposition.

THE INFLUENTIAL LEADER

184

Can your spending be justified by the
benefit it brings to family, friends,
neighbors, and above all, to the work
of God and to a hurting humanity?

THE WACKERSBERG CONNECTION

185

Close a good explanation with a powerful
challenge. It puts people on notice. It
gives them a motivated reason to act.

NOTES FROM MY DIARY

186

Even if you're asking someone into your office only for five minutes, make sure your aims are clearly defined. Meetings serve no purpose unless you have something to discuss and decide.

THE SEVEN SECRETS OF SUCCESSFUL
BUSINESS RELATIONSHIPS

187

Faithful stewardship of life leads to complete fulfillment, the enlarged life; failure in stewardship impoverishes, robbing life of its potential.

THE STEWARD

188

Too many Christians create dichotomies
in their lifestyles. While they call upon
God to direct and protect them in all
other personal affairs, they lock the
same God out of their financial affairs.
When we do this, we rob ourselves of
the wisdom and resources of Heaven.

10 COMMANDMENTS FOR FINANCIAL
FREEDOM AND CRISIS SURVIVAL

189

If you're laden down with things
that do not enrich your life, you
have to ask yourself if those things
are in fact impoverishing you.

EXPONENTIAL

190

Having a fast car or running a big
company doesn't make other people like
you or trust you or want to do what you say.

THE INFLUENTIAL LEADER

191

You sin against the leaders, the managers,
and the enterprise when you put managers
in leadership positions and when you
saddle leaders with a lot of minutiae.

NOTES FROM MY DIARY

192

You can never ask too much. You can never think too broadly, too grandly. All you must do is ensure that the thinking, the asking, and the imagining focus on glorifying God.

EXPONENTIAL

193

Do your own thinking.

HOW TO WIN OVER WORRY

194

Few things, though, will damage
your reputation more than letting
other people feel small.

THE SEVEN SECRETS OF SUCCESSFUL
BUSINESS RELATIONSHIPS

195

I do not believe that anyone should
exercise leadership over others until
he or she has first learned to accept
authority from another person.

THE INFLUENTIAL LEADER

196

The quality of stewardship (or lack of it) reveals graphically the level of one's spiritual relationship with God.

THE STEWARD

197

Every man has some good points, but Jesus Christ had them all.

EXPONENTIAL

198

All people are created unequal. The
Lord gave different amounts of talents
to different people. It's incumbent
upon the person to do according to
what he or she has, not according
to what he or she has not.

NOTES FROM MY DIARY

199

When you are tired, admit it to
yourself and get out of public view.
Get your rest. Let people see you
only when you are vigorous.

THE INFLUENTIAL LEADER

200

Faith operates only in the gap between
what the Lord lays upon your heart—
and what you're capable of in your
own strength and resources at the
time He lays that insight upon you.

NOTES FROM MY DIARY

201

You choose to worry—or you choose not to.

HOW TO WIN OVER WORRY

202

Leaders have to thrive on ambiguity.

THE INFLUENTIAL LEADER

203

When dealing with hotel and airline staff, dispense with the personal note but inject real feeling into your "Good morning." In my experience, about one customer in twenty rouses himself to do this. Believe me, it makes a difference.

THE SEVEN SECRETS OF SUCCESSFUL
BUSINESS RELATIONSHIPS

204

Impatience leads to anxiety over small
setbacks and to loss of long-term vision.

10 COMMANDMENTS FOR FINANCIAL
FREEDOM AND CRISIS SURVIVAL

205

Are you assigning to your stated values
and goals a proportion of your time
commensurate with their importance?

NOTES FROM MY DIARY

206

A weakness of many who occupy positions
of leadership today is their readiness
to bail out under pressure. When
you talk with them intimately, you
discover they have already made plans
to abandon their leadership position.

THE INFLUENTIAL LEADER

207

If you want a friend, be one.

BE CAREFUL WHAT YOU
CALL IMPOSSIBLE

208

It's easier to cool down a red-hot cinder
than to warm up a dead corpse.

NOTES FROM MY DIARY

209

Can you really expect our Lord's
optimum blessing on your life and work
if His priority is not your priority?

EXPONENTIAL

210

The influential leader does not
neglect family responsibilities or
use work as a way of escaping from
difficult relationships at home.

THE INFLUENTIAL LEADER

211

All things being equal, I find that what
distinguishes achievers can be enumerated
as follows: (1) They act; (2) they act
without procrastination; (3) while not
always making the right decisions,
they always make decisions right.

NOTES FROM MY DIARY

212

Expect nothing, and you'll
get exactly nothing.

THE SEVEN SECRETS OF SUCCESSFUL
BUSINESS RELATIONSHIPS

213

When a man is properly related to God,
he has within himself all the ingredients
necessary to provide security, joy, and
peace, regardless of external conditions.

HOW TO WIN OVER WORRY

214

Solve today's challenges today. Leave
tomorrow's challenges for tomorrow.

THE INFLUENTIAL LEADER

215

Dramatic entrances at five minutes past
the appointed hour don't recommend
you as a busy person—they confirm
you as rude and unprofessional.

THE SEVEN SECRETS OF SUCCESSFUL
BUSINESS RELATIONSHIPS

216

The Bible does not condemn money.
It's the love of money—making
money more important in your life
than Jesus Christ—that the Bible
declares to be the root of all evil.

THE STEWARD

217

What one leader strives to gain, the next
is afraid to lose. After pioneers develop a
track record, the subsequent leadership
often becomes conservative and protective.

EXPONENTIAL

218

Having authority and liking to hold
power are two quite different things.

THE INFLUENTIAL LEADER

219

Is it not sad that people who claim to be
disciples of the living God show less daring,
less faith, less abandon toward objectives
God lays upon their hearts than secular
people do in the world of commerce?

NOTES FROM MY DIARY

220

You can have true inner authority
only if you are at peace with your
inner self—if you understand that
you are a person worth following.

THE INFLUENTIAL LEADER

221

Most people put more energy into network
development than they do into friendship.

THE WACKERSBERG CONNECTION

222

God doesn't read the *Financial Times* or the *Wall Street Journal,* nor is His net worth affected by the price of gold. God operates independently of the Dow Jones and the international economic indicators. And He never suffers a financial crisis.

10 COMMANDMENTS FOR FINANCIAL
FREEDOM AND CRISIS SURVIVAL

223

Leaders who are completely immersed in their life-work, who with singleness of mind pursue their mission, tend to exhibit a greater authority than others.

THE INFLUENTIAL LEADER

224

Humility is not denying God's
special blessings. It is simply
recognizing who is the source.

NOTES FROM MY DIARY

225

Much has been written about the first
four minutes of a relationship. By far the
most crucial interaction, though, occurs
in the first four seconds. At that "point
of entry" you give out an explosion of
signals, verbal and nonverbal, that set
the tone for everything that follows.

THE SEVEN SECRETS OF SUCCESSFUL
BUSINESS RELATIONSHIPS

226

One of my hobbies is reading books on salesmanship. I have a collection of more than fifty. Without exception, each book on salesmanship underscores enthusiasm as an essential quality for success.

HOW TO WIN OVER WORRY

227

Without a strong vision, you will end up going over the same decisions again and again because you are constantly in two minds and tempted to change direction.

THE INFLUENTIAL LEADER

228

When you pray, do you believe that
He is able? When you undertake an
assignment, whether it be in business
or home or church, do you, deep down
in your soul, believe that He is able
to see you through to victory? Or are
you a timid "I hope so" believer?

EXPONENTIAL

229

The Bible says "Lot pitched his tent toward
Sodom." When you pitch your tent
toward Sodom, it's only a matter of time
until you're living in downtown Sodom.

NOTES FROM MY DIARY

230

Picture yourself meeting your future child
as your own contemporary. What kind of
person would you want him or her to be?

BE CAREFUL WHAT YOU
CALL IMPOSSIBLE

231

Limit your self-disclosure to a few
trusted people—your husband or wife,
a close friend or mentor. Otherwise,
keep your thoughts to yourself.

THE INFLUENTIAL LEADER

232

Money can buy you happiness only if
you spend the money on someone else.

NOTES FROM MY DIARY

233

The majority of prosperous businessmen
will burn up fifty to eighty hours a week
to create wealth and devote less than
one hour a month to the philanthropic
distribution of any part of it.

THE STEWARD

234

I knew that I could choose to worry
or choose not to worry. It was my
choice. And I preferred winning over
worry to having worry win over me.

HOW TO WIN OVER WORRY

235

Show as much respect for the person who
answers the telephone in an office as you
do for the president of the company.

THE INFLUENTIAL LEADER

236

Add together all the time lost waiting
for key people to arrive at business
meetings, and you'd soon be at the
end of the next millennium.

THE SEVEN SECRETS OF SUCCESSFUL
BUSINESS RELATIONSHIPS

237

How can we justify our willingness to trust
other men, the marketplace, the military,
the physician, and yet distrust God?

THE STEWARD

238

How can you move in the direction
that your thought repels?

EXPONENTIAL

239

If leaders can't handle ambiguity—
can't anticipate it, can't ride it—they
are not providing leadership.

THE INFLUENTIAL LEADER

240

All great achievements begin with
the imagination. A passion to
make money without a legitimate
reason for its use will fail.

EXPONENTIAL

241

Too many people act before they
understand what they are acting on.

NOTES FROM MY DIARY

242

A network of friends is an altogether
more powerful entity than a network
of acquaintances. It runs deeper and
carries the potential of stronger, more
permanent, and more committed
linkages. It invests influence.

THE WACKERSBERG CONNECTION

243

Your greatest opportunities will
often appear cleverly disguised
as insurmountable problems.

NOTES FROM MY DIARY

244

When you refuse to make your own decisions, someone else makes the decisions for you. The men and women who have made the world great had no safety net to catch them.

THE INFLUENTIAL LEADER

245

Avoid passivity like the plague.

HOW TO WIN OVER WORRY

246

Nothing will ever be attempted if all possible obstacles must first be overcome.

THE INFLUENTIAL LEADER

247

Christian love doesn't pour itself irrecoverably into a bottomless pit of another's needs. Like bread on the water, it returns.

THE WACKERSBERG CONNECTION

248

I believe that worry is an underlying
condition of American society—
and probably global society also.
Not everyone suffers from clinical
depression or psychosis. But everyone,
at some time, will worry.

HOW TO WIN OVER WORRY

249

The people who follow you don't
always see the bigger picture.

THE INFLUENTIAL LEADER

250

No tree grows into the stratosphere.

NOTES FROM MY DIARY

251

God's grace, God's mercy, God's
provisions come to us day by day as
we need them. You can count on it.

EXPONENTIAL

252

Having insight achieves nothing
if you refuse to act on it.

NOTES FROM MY DIARY

253

A company without a clear vision is a
company doomed to fail. Business leaders
need to know where they are going, and
they need to be able to communicate
that vision in visionary decision making.

THE INFLUENTIAL LEADER

254

God blesses those who keep on keeping on.

NOTES FROM MY DIARY

255

Is your imagination under divine control or have you finally shut down your dream machine? Have you yielded to the taunts and the negative thinking of people around you who have never accomplished much themselves?

EXPONENTIAL

256

We are all on the same level when it comes
to time. We each have sixty minutes in
each hour and twenty-four hours in each
day. How we organize them is up to us.

HOW TO WIN OVER WORRY

257

I believe that worthy visions are a gift of
God—even visions for business or politics.

THE INFLUENTIAL LEADER

258

The body as a whole can achieve
benefits the individual members can
never realize. Cooperation enriches
and accelerates achievement.

BE CAREFUL WHAT YOU
CALL IMPOSSIBLE

259

Successful deal-making, as well as
successful management, depends upon
a keen observation of the interests and
characteristics of those you work with.

THE SEVEN SECRETS OF SUCCESSFUL
BUSINESS RELATIONSHIPS

260

Do you have the humility to support
what you can't dominate?

THE STEWARD

261

Goals should be measurable in two
ways. First, by specifying what you
will accomplish. Second, by specifying
when you will accomplish it.

THE INFLUENTIAL LEADER

262

Democracy cannot be solid and
secure when citizens, from the leaders
all the way down to the man in the
street, no longer trust each other.

NOTES FROM MY DIARY

263

Enthusiasm is like steam. It pressurizes,
empowers, impels action. Many
people never become enthusiastic
over anything, therefore they never
achieve anything. Their lives become
idle and negative and worrisome.

HOW TO WIN OVER WORRY

264

Even when others know you're busy,
failure to respond quickly to calls
will give the impression you regard
their business as low-priority.

THE SEVEN SECRETS OF SUCCESSFUL
BUSINESS RELATIONSHIPS

265

Embrace a goal that stretches you to
the limit, that captures the essence of
your heart's desire, and then get down
to the nitty-gritty process of charting a
course to get there. The higher you aim,
the further you will go—every time.

THE INFLUENTIAL LEADER

266

Abilities won't survive neglect. You develop
your abilities, or they decay and die.

THE STEWARD

267

If two people agree on everything,
one person is totally unnecessary.

NOTES FROM MY DIARY

268

A friend is one who knows all about you,
sees your faults, and loves you anyway.

THE WACKERSBERG CONNECTION

269

Writing crystallizes your thoughts
and makes your ideas specific.

THE INFLUENTIAL LEADER

270

Although unhappiness and discontent
are powerful motivators, they
cannot give direction. Goals can.

BE CAREFUL WHAT YOU
CALL IMPOSSIBLE

271

Mediocrity is a man with Beethoven's
capabilities clanging away on a Jew's harp.

NOTES FROM MY DIARY

272

Develop daily the discipline of habitually moving forward in some way toward your God-honoring target. Enrich your life by making God's will your dream.

EXPONENTIAL

273

I cannot insist too strongly that setting goals is not a one-time exercise. It is an ongoing discipline. Life is not static—it is dynamic. Your goals must be constantly modified. Therefore, you need to stay on top of your goals so that a changing environment will not catch you by surprise.

THE INFLUENTIAL LEADER

274

No one can be right with God and
wrong on the money question.

NOTES FROM MY DIARY

275

The person who never wonders at anything
never does anything wonderful.

HOW TO WIN OVER WORRY

276

A relationship that consists of an exchange of cardboard once every twelve months isn't going anywhere. You're letting the other person know you're still alive—and that's it.

THE SEVEN SECRETS OF SUCCESSFUL
BUSINESS RELATIONSHIPS

277

If goal setting is so wonderful, why don't more people do it? Probably the main reason is that effective goal setting takes effort. It takes determination. It takes commitment. And it also takes an ability to put aside your fears.

THE INFLUENTIAL LEADER

278

It's too easy to be in a rush, driven by
a relentless work schedule, and allow
insufficient food, insufficient exercise, and
insufficient sleep to erode your effectiveness.
It's always an easy excuse to say you're busy.
But being busy can boil down to a state of
perpetual nervous tension—a biochemical
high you can't come down from until
circumstances get the better of you.

HOW TO WIN OVER WORRY

279

Delegate, but don't abdicate.

THE SEVEN SECRETS OF SUCCESSFUL
BUSINESS RELATIONSHIPS

280

Give God the glory
for all your blessings.

THE STEWARD

281

Too often we confuse leadership with
popularity, power, showmanship, or
wisdom in long-range planning. None
of these can substitute for leadership
that connects personally to others.
Nor will any be as effective.

THE INFLUENTIAL LEADER

282

People who don't understand
faith identify faith as risk.

NOTES FROM MY DIARY

283

God is a God of friendship. Jesus is "a
friend that sticks closer than a brother." So
make a habit of thanking Him for those
with whom He has put you in touch.

THE WACKERSBERG CONNECTION

284

Know your business. Stay in close touch
with it. Meet the spiritual as well as the
material needs of your employees.

THE STEWARD

285

Putting love in your decision making has
nothing to do with your emotions. How
you feel is irrelevant. The love consists in
the decision itself, not in how you felt when
you made the decision. I can feel sorry
for victims of an earthquake, but a far
better barometer of my concern for them
is whether I support efforts to help them.

THE INFLUENTIAL LEADER

286

Believe God, and expect results.

10 COMMANDMENTS FOR FINANCIAL
FREEDOM AND CRISIS SURVIVAL

287

Impression without
expression leads to depression.

NOTES FROM MY DIARY

288

With every option you choose,
there will be somebody waiting to tell
you what a big mistake you've made.

HOW TO WIN OVER WORRY

289

Love is active, never passive. It demands
expression. Also, love is transitive. It
demands an object. Love is unerringly
practical. It serves and it sacrifices. And
in doing so, it cultivates in others the
motivation to work hard and reach goals.

THE INFLUENTIAL LEADER

290

Delegation is a good thing. As my dear old friend Eddie Lieberman said, "If you don't delegate, you don't have an organization."

EXPONENTIAL

291

I believe that God deals with a nation according to the behavior of His people.

NOTES FROM MY DIARY

292

Without a variety of interests, you will
not keep anyone's attention for long.

HOW TO WIN OVER WORRY

293

You take care of your body by visiting
the gym. Your spirit needs the same
help. Only by understanding that God
loves, forgives, and accepts you can
you achieve a healthy self-esteem.

THE INFLUENTIAL LEADER

294

If your talk dominates the conversation,
the other party may find you far
less interesting than you think.

THE SEVEN SECRETS OF SUCCESSFUL
BUSINESS RELATIONSHIPS

295

Rarely have I heard men say, "God has
so wonderfully blessed my business. I've
prospered in a greater way than I could
have imagined. I'd like to underwrite
at least one half of this project."

THE STEWARD

296

God bless those whose vision
stretches beyond the horizon.

EXPONENTIAL

297

Unlike the mechanic who deals primarily
with things, or the mathematician who
deals primarily with ideas, the leader
deals with people. And people respond
well, and give of their best, only when
they know they are treated with love.

THE INFLUENTIAL LEADER

298

Self-delusion is a natural result
of trying to present ourselves as
something other than we really are.

NOTES FROM MY DIARY

299

There's nothing virtuous
about being unprepared.

THE SEVEN SECRETS OF SUCCESSFUL
BUSINESS RELATIONSHIPS

300

The trouble with many people is that
instead of looking to Jesus they are
looking to tomorrow, waiting for
circumstances to turn and favor them.
What a tragic waste of opportunity.

HOW TO WIN OVER WORRY

301

The loveless, self-centered power-holder
will try to get his way by creating
factions, skillfully fomenting conflict,
and keeping others off balance. This
modus operandi defeats its own
purposes. By working for harmony, the
influential leader may lose some votes, but
ultimately he will take the organization
in a direction that benefits everyone.

THE INFLUENTIAL LEADER

302

Relate every area of your life, personal
and professional, to the will of God.

THE STEWARD

303

The first law of negotiation is
that doormats get walked on.

THE SEVEN SECRETS OF SUCCESSFUL
BUSINESS RELATIONSHIPS

304

Will Jesus, who gave His life to
save, be pleased that professing
Christians have given billions to
train the head and damn the soul?

NOTES FROM MY DIARY

305

You gain nothing by letting your
frustration boil over into anger with others.

THE INFLUENTIAL LEADER

306

Freedom permits you to either create
wings and fly or forge a ball and chain
and enter into self-imposed slavery.

NOTES FROM MY DIARY

307

Anyone who achieves by bringing a vision
to life through synergism—that is, through
the combined enthusiasm and effort of
colleagues—chisels a name into history.

THE WACKERSBERG CONNECTION

308

It is a basic law of human nature
that you will feel as you think and
act. You cannot think fearfully and act
courageously. Conversely, you cannot
think courageously and act fearfully.

HOW TO WIN OVER WORRY

309

Love makes leadership influential. There
is no limit on the number of such leaders
business organizations can accommodate.

THE INFLUENTIAL LEADER

310

Take care what you let into your mind.

HOW TO WIN OVER WORRY

311

The man who can speak can have virtually any position he wants—especially if he has brains and charm to go with it.

NOTES FROM MY DIARY

312

There is no reason for you to
conform to stereotypes that belong
to a previous generation.

BE CAREFUL WHAT YOU
CALL IMPOSSIBLE

313

If you hope to rise to your potential as
a leader, you'll do well to meet criticism
with tranquility and pleasantness.

THE INFLUENTIAL LEADER

314

Do you stick by your friends when they are in trouble or need, or when their reputation could be an embarrassment to you?

THE WACKERSBERG CONNECTION

315

Prominence and prosperity do not of themselves improve character nor honor God.

NOTES FROM MY DIARY

316

Don't mistake grumbling
for spiritual heroism.

HOW TO WIN OVER WORRY

317

If you congratulate yourself for
being humble, you are probably not
as humble as you like to think.

THE INFLUENTIAL LEADER

318

Jesus never complained
about the weight of His cross.

HOW TO WIN OVER WORRY

319

Praise the performance, not the person.

THE SEVEN SECRETS OF SUCCESSFUL
BUSINESS RELATIONSHIPS

320

People who never take time to think never
master the control of their own minds.

NOTES FROM MY DIARY

321

Regular exercise takes discipline.
Maintaining an organized workplace
takes discipline. Getting out of bed
on time takes discipline. Discipline is
necessary to have a healthy diet. You may
think the small things don't matter, but
a lack of discipline in little things will
affect your ability to maintain discipline
in big things. Those who are disciplined
in small things tend to be disciplined
in big things as well. By contrast, those
who lack discipline in minor details
will lack discipline everywhere.

THE INFLUENTIAL LEADER

322

In my view, the most accurate barometer
of a church's vitality is what it does in the
matter of evangelism, not only at home but
also "to the uttermost parts of the earth."

NOTES FROM MY DIARY

323

Incomplete obedience to God's command
is disobedience. Careless obedience is dead
obedience; the heart is gone out of it.

EXPONENTIAL

324

What are you doing better this
week than you did last week?

NOTES FROM MY DIARY

325

Because the humble leader makes
no pretense of being self-sufficient
or knowing all the answers, he is
able to draw insights from others.

THE INFLUENTIAL LEADER

326

I cannot think of any great decision
that was made by a large crowd.

NOTES FROM MY DIARY

327

How often do you contact your friends
when you desire nothing from them?

THE WACKERSBERG CONNECTION

328

Stir up your gift, your abilities, as you
would stir up the fire under the embers.

THE STEWARD

329

Prayer makes you efficient. This fact ought
also to induce a greater interest in prayer.

HOW TO WIN OVER WORRY

330

The person who continually says,
"I must not do this, I must not do
that…" actually undermines himself
by focusing on what he doesn't want to
do. Thus he etches in the cortex of his
brain the very thing he wants to get
away from. He should be visualizing
future success, not present failures.

THE INFLUENTIAL LEADER

331

If you own forty suits and you wear only
six of them, you're paying storage for
thirty-four suits. You no more possess
them than if you had never bought them.

EXPONENTIAL

332

Money is a commodity, nothing
more. It has no intrinsic value. It can
accomplish great good, and it can wreck
lives. It all depends on how it's used.

NOTES FROM MY DIARY

333

Each of us has a different combination
of gifts, a different set of God-given
connections and friends. Each of
us makes his own investment.

THE WACKERSBERG CONNECTION

334

Leadership requires a cool head. While others respond to what they see, the influential leader responds to what is really happening—the direction of the long-term trends.

THE INFLUENTIAL LEADER

335

My cousin Leo said to his father one day, "Dad, why is it when you give your testimony in church, you tell what a bad fellow you were, but when you're talking to us, you tell us what a good boy you were?"

NOTES FROM MY DIARY

336

Long before my financial crisis hit,
I'd learned how to win over worry.

HOW TO WIN OVER WORRY

337

A good conversationalist is
someone who's interested in the
world where the other person lives.

THE SEVEN SECRETS OF SUCCESSFUL
BUSINESS RELATIONSHIPS

338

Goal setting is just a healthier way to live.

THE INFLUENTIAL LEADER

339

Often I think of Jesus' question, "Are there not twelve hours in a day?" By that I think He was suggesting there's enough time every day to do everything God wants you to do if you simply redeem the time.

THE STEWARD

340

Your life will never attain optimum
significance apart from total obedience to
the Lord's command to take the Gospel
to the entire world. That's categorical.

EXPONENTIAL

341

Faith is a gift of God. So says the Word
of God. Air too is a gift of God. It will
do you no good unless you breathe.

NOTES FROM MY DIARY

342

An attitude of self-control develops
strong character. It never counts its
companions. Nor does it judge itself
by the number of its admirers.

THE INFLUENTIAL LEADER

343

One unique characteristic about successful
investors: they don't listen to the crowd.

NOTES FROM MY DIARY

344

Remember that unjust criticism is often a backhanded compliment. It often indicates that you have excited the interest, jealousy, and envy of the critic. As the old adage goes, "No one ever kicks a dead dog."

HOW TO WIN OVER WORRY

345

No pharmacy has enough medicine to kill a single germ or ease a single pain unless you take the medicine.

NOTES FROM MY DIARY

346

The real test of a leader's courage and ability to stand alone comes in times of crisis. When the stock price is sinking. When the credit is running out. When people are starting to lose their nerve. A crisis removes all subterfuge, double-talk, and posturing. At such times, you must have self-control. If you don't, collapse will quickly follow.

THE INFLUENTIAL LEADER

347

All contacts and friendships are God's gift.

THE WACKERSBERG CONNECTION

348

I used to take great pride, as a young man, in sleeping only four or five hours. I had read that John Wesley arose at four o'clock every morning for his devotions. I started doing the same. But nobody told me that Wesley went to bed at eight o'clock every night!

NOTES FROM MY DIARY

349

Spiritually speaking, most of us can much better afford adversity than prosperity.

HOW TO WIN OVER WORRY

350

False humility rarely works because most people can detect pride within seconds, no matter how hard you try to camouflage it.

THE INFLUENTIAL LEADER

351

For your own peace of mind, excel in at least one thing.

HOW TO WIN OVER WORRY

352

One day in the late 1800s, a lady shopping in the Wanamaker store in Philadelphia asked the clerk, "Is this cloth genuine linen?" The clerk responded, "It was before evangelist D.L. Moody came to town. Now, madam, I am obliged to tell you that it's fake!" That's revival.

NOTES FROM MY DIARY

353

Do you want to be the richest man in the cemetery?

THE WACKERSBERG CONNECTION

354

Self-control works best when you make
your decisions ahead of time—and live
according to those decisions. In effect,
you are writing your rules for living.
Writing and internalizing such rules not
only strengthens your leadership, but
also gives you greater self-confidence
and serenity. Having the power of habit
on your side confers great advantage.

THE INFLUENTIAL LEADER

355

Love establishes contact, trust, reciprocity;
it throws open the door to opportunities,
unimagined and previously unperceived.

THE WACKERSBERG CONNECTION

356

All institutions begin from the top
down, not from the bottom up.

NOTES FROM MY DIARY

357

I don't know of anyone with serious money
who hasn't a capacity for relationships—
that's how integral friendship is to business.

THE SEVEN SECRETS OF SUCCESSFUL
BUSINESS RELATIONSHIPS

358

The commercials tell you repeatedly that
freedom comes not from self-control but
from self-indulgence—the next holiday,
the next expensive dress, the next drink. In
reality, unrestrained self-indulgence leads
to slavery, both financial and spiritual.

THE INFLUENTIAL LEADER

359

The more I commit myself to
the Lord in the morning, the less
I have to confess at night.

HOW TO WIN OVER WORRY

360

Never swinging the bat will
never win a ball game.

NOTES FROM MY DIARY

361

Do you put your money into
things or into people?

THE WACKERSBERG CONNECTION

362

Self-discipline produces freedom
by shutting off useless options.

THE INFLUENTIAL LEADER

363

The person who cannot control
himself ultimately becomes the
slave of the person who can.

THE INFLUENTIAL LEADER

364

The only motive that God ever
gave for a person to give money
was the motive of self-interest.

NOTES FROM MY DIARY

365

He who sees the invisible
can do the impossible.

EXPONENTIAL